# growing giving

By Brenda Babitz

A Guide to Securing
Private Support for
Your Community College

Council for Advancement and Support of Education (CASE) is the professional organization for advancement professionals at all levels who work in alumni relations, communications, development and advancement services.

CASE offers high-quality training, information resources, and a wide variety of books and publications for advancement professionals.

For more information on CASE or a copy of our books catalog, visit *www.case.org*, or call (202) 328-5900.

Book design: TFW Design Inc.
Art director: Angela Carpenter Gildner
Cover illustration: ©Leon Zernitsky/Images.com

COUNCIL FOR
ADVANCEMENT AND
SUPPORT OF EDUCATION
1307 New York Avenue, NW
Suite 1000
Washington, DC 20005-4701
*www.case.org*

CASE EUROPE
5-11 Worship Street
London EC2A 2BH
United Kingdom

CASE ASIA-PACIFIC
20 Lower Kent Ridge Road
Singapore 119080

| *Foreword* | *Fundraising at the Top of the Star* |

Brenda Babitz was one of the first people we called when we began editing the volume *Successful Approaches to Fund Raising and Development* (2003). After reading her book, you'll understand why. She has her finger on the pulse of one of the most influential trends in community colleges: private fundraising.

Fundraising is front and center in conversations among community and technical college CEOs–and for good reason. Research and practice show that fundraising is fast becoming one of the key reasons why presidents and chancellors are hired, fired, and rewarded. This isn't surprising in the least. Fundraising is a fast-flowing confluent in the "third wave" transforming community colleges.

The first wave began in 1949 with the Truman Commission on Higher Education. In the decades that followed, we saw the merging of junior colleges and vocational-technical institutes. It was the inception of the comprehensive community college, with a focus on both academics and vocational training. Wave two saw the flood of workforce development further change the engagement and outreach of our institutions in our communities. In the 1980s, business and industry training centers, contract training, industry certifications, and significantly expanded workforce training fundamentally transformed most community colleges' operations. We became home to Cisco Network Academies, MCSE training centers, TQM consulting services, and more.

The third wave began to rise over the last six years. While CEO of the League for Innovation in the Community College, I saw our national trends surveys of college CEOs suddenly reflect a changing expectation. The CEOs were increasingly being asked to take a more aggressive role in advancing their institutions—particularly in improving institutional funding. Shrinking state budgets, fluctuating federal budgets, and increasing program costs conspired to make this role a critical necessity for most community college presidents.

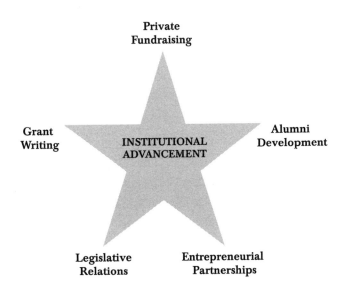

In the age of this third wave, college leaders at all levels are being asked to bring together a host of strategies to advance their institutions' missions. We can think about these major areas of advancement as the five points of the institutional advancement star: (1) private fundraising, (2) alumni development, (3) grant writing, (4) legislative relations, and (5) entrepreneurial partnerships.

Each of the star's points works synergistically with the others, and each point deserves a volume in and of itself. However, it is private fundraising that is arguably the newest to our field. As you read and learn about the current demographic projections, you'll find that private fundraising holds the most powerful potential to support our work significantly. Finally, it is often private fundraising that brings together conversations surrounding the other elements of advancement. Our fundraising efforts challenge us to reach out to our alumni, build relationships with key figures who can impact our ability to win grants, and successfully support legislation. In addition, it opens the doors to other partnerships that expand our reach and enhance our endowments.

*Growing Giving* belongs at the top of your institutional advancement star. In the pages that follow, you'll get a clear picture of the opportunity, the operational elements, and strategies for securing the support necessary to serve your students.

All the best as you take this rewarding journey!

**Mark David Milliron**

Suanne Davis Roueche Endowed Fellow
Senior Lecturer, and Director

National Institute of Staff and
Organizational Development

College of Education
University of Texas at Austin

# *Table of Contents*

# *Introduction*

I was eager to begin my community college advancement career at Monroe Community College in Rochester, NY, in May 1990, but it was not until I attended my first commencement ceremony four weeks later that I realized what a wise choice I had made. As I watched graduates of every age, ethnicity, and walk of life receive their degrees, I witnessed the "American Dream" coming true at MCC.

With mothers, fathers, grandparents, children, spouses, siblings, and employers cheering in the stands, I saw that MCC was changing lives—one student at a time. This community college—like the nearly 1,300 community colleges nationwide—was in the business of transforming both people and communities.

During these past 16 years, I have had the pleasure of telling this story time and again. It is fulfilling to participate in the rapid changes taking place in the community college world and to help others recognize the vital role that public higher education plays in this country.

I have gained a special appreciation for the new challenges and opportunities that are emerging and the increasingly critical need for private-sector funding. Now is the time for community colleges to take their place at the fundraising table.

If we focus and follow the lessons learned at four-year institutions, we can reach the right audiences and, ultimately, benefit those who want to better themselves through education. Philanthropy, after all, makes the world go around—we all are its beneficiaries.

**Brenda Babitz**
President
Monroe Community College Foundation
May 2007

# *Growing Giving*

With economic stagnation and diminished tax revenues depleting the coffers of state and local governments nationwide, America's community colleges must look beyond the public sector to fund their educational missions.

As such, community college presidents and trustees are turning increasingly to college foundations, assigning advancement officers the task of developing new, external sources of income within the private sector. Whether in the form of gifts or grants, private support is needed to help bridge the gap between what public funding, at best, can provide and what excellence in community-based education and training now demands.

The challenge facing community college advancement officers has never been greater or more consequential. But while the vast majority of community colleges now have foundations, the impact of most operations and the revenues they generate remain negligible.

*Growing Giving* offers proven ways to grow relationships—internally and externally—and identify giving opportunities based on benchmarks achieved by other advancement operations. The specific recommendations included in *Growing Giving* are designed to enhance the productivity, effectiveness, and bottom-line returns of community college advancement efforts.

# *Some General Observations*

Beginning our journey with general observations from successful advancement programs will help you identify areas of particular interest that will move your organization forward. The following lessons are explored further in this book:

- Your foundation must be viewed by senior administrators, faculty, and staff as an integral part of the institution and its future.

- The more a community college emphasizes private philanthropy, the more it establishes expectations among constituents.

- People give to your college because its mission is consistent with their values.

- The longer the advancement officer's tenure, the greater the opportunity for prospecting and relationship building.

- Surprise gifts are rarely surprises. It is much more likely that the donor has had a long and trusting relationship with an institution.

- Only 10 percent of receiving a gift is asking for it—the other 90 percent is preparation.

- There is a direct, positive correlation between the number of advancement staff and the amount of dollars raised.

- Advancement staff are increasingly involved in asking for a gift and thus must be able to articulate institutional priorities.

- The notion of philanthropy should be introduced the first day students arrive on your campus—so they will consider giving back.

- Students who have participated in extracurricular activities are more likely to contribute when they become alumni.

# Part I
*Philanthropy:
A Changing Landscape*

Almost every aspect of American life—from the arts to health care, social programs to education—has been strengthened, advanced, and enriched by private-sector involvement. In fact, our country practiced philanthropy long before we became a nation. John Winthrop, the first governor of Massachusetts, urged the rich to recognize their responsibilities to the poor. As early as the mid-1600s then-Harvard College began raising money for educational purposes. Its first president, Henry Dunster, sought gifts for capital improvements and fellowships. Benjamin Franklin gave impetus to educational philanthropy with the founding of the Philadelphia Academy (later called the University of Pennsylvania) and the Philadelphia Hospital. With a challenge grant, he was able to receive subscriptions that far exceeded his 4,000-pound goal.

While Franklin gave philanthropy a uniquely American character, it took the wealth and genius of Andrew Carnegie, Henry Ford, and John D. Rockefeller to transform philanthropy in America and in our communities.

Pressured by a need for charitable giving following World War I, the United States enacted laws that provided tax relief in exchange for personal giving. Perhaps prompted by these tax breaks—and inspired by those who wanted to create a better world—giving in this country has continued to increase steadily, from an estimated $1.7 billion in 1921 to more than

$260 billion in 2005. According to *Giving USA 2005*, giving to education has grown by 162 percent since 1984, "far exceeding the 62 percent growth in disposable personal income in the same period."

Looking toward the coming years, the 2005 study *Wealth in America*, conducted by Northern Trust (*www.northerntrust.com*), found that nearly half of America's most affluent households plan to increase their charitable giving. Seventy-one percent of the people surveyed responded that "donating time and/or money to charities or nonprofit organization is embedded in their family life," and nearly half (47 percent) want to be personally involved in the organizations to which they donate. Religious and social service organizations topped the list of donation recipients (58 and 52 percent respectively), followed by colleges and universities (41 percent). Paul G. Schervich and John Havens of the Center for Wealth and Philanthropy at Boston College project that by 2052, $31 to $41 trillion will be transferred from one generation to the next in this country.

American philanthropy is also entering a period of unprecedented change, with leaders of today's information revolution putting their own mark on the social sector. While Carnegie, Ford, and Rockefeller created the private foundations that underpin today's philanthropic and nonprofit work, their modern counterparts are bringing entrepreneurial acumen to philanthropy, demanding results and carefully assessing their social investments. According to *eJournal USA: Society & Values*, "The nature and practice of philanthropy in the United States is currently experiencing a spectacular change fueled mostly by growth in size and character. It is, in many respects, a time of optimism and creativity as people explore new systems for bringing private wealth back to the community from which it was derived to benefit the public good."

As philanthropy is reinventing itself, community colleges must also begin to transform their advancement programs. Those institutions that are proactive have much to gain: empowering successive generations of students, stimulating economic growth and productivity, and fostering the spirit of community itself.

## *The Case for Community Colleges*

Beginning with Joliet Junior College in Illinois at the turn of the 19th century, community colleges have spread across the United States to meet the increasing demand for public higher education. Originally funded exclusively with public dollars, the concept of "fundraising" was not part of the original design. It is only within the past 20 years that community colleges have become more entrepreneurial and cognizant of what it takes to secure philanthropic support.

Shrinking external funding streams and growing institutional worth have given rise to the creation of institutional foundations, which serve as the primary vehicles to solicit, accept, and manage private funds on behalf of the community colleges they serve. These foundations, functioning much like development offices at private institutions, have been given the responsibility of engaging the private sector. In 2002, the *Community College Journal* reported that community colleges across the nation "are implementing strategies to solicit support"–and that some have been more successful than others.

Recognizing that community college fundraising is still small in terms of relative impact, the Ford Foundation funded a 2004 study to learn how Americans perceive community colleges and how more support could be raised for these institutions. Entitled "Expanding Opportunity," the study recommends that "communications to support community colleges need to aim first at increasing awareness of the urgent need for more funding for community colleges, then to identify, enlighten and fire up the natural allies."

Given the lack of long-standing programs and active research protocols in community college fundraising, advancement officers are wise to rely on the lessons learned by the foundations of large four-year public colleges and universities.

Now is the perfect time to create opportunities to identify, nurture, and direct a significant portion of private funding to our institutions. Fortunately, the private sector is beginning to appreciate the case for America's community colleges:

- We rapidly adapt to the changing needs of students and communities.
- We are committed to educational access.
- We have a growing impact on community well-being.
- We have the capacity to meet the workforce-training needs of businesses, both large and small.

## *Private Support for Public Institutions*

Originally funded by public support, tuition and fees, some forward-thinking community colleges did engage in fundraising early on, although primarily for scholarships. However, until this decade, the generation of significant private revenues, while welcomed, has not been a priority for most community college presidents. As diminishing government support, changeable student enrollment, and higher operating costs alter the landscape, community college presidents are adopting a new perspective. Forward-thinking presidents are turning to their foundations as an important revenue source to offset the impact of budget cuts and sustain educational excellence and accessibility.

John Lippincott, president of the Council for Advancement and Support of Education, forecasts, "Community colleges are poised for big windfalls in the years to come." These anticipated "windfalls" cannot happen soon enough. Across our nation today, the baby-boom echoes are reaching college age; a new wave of immigrants and first-generation students look to higher education as the springboard to a better life; and millions of workers face the need to upgrade skills or be left among the downsized.

This confluence of demographic and economic trends is placing unprecedented demands on our institutions. Equally challenging, it comes at a time of economic uncertainty, a volatile stock market, and a decline at every level of government in the capacity to fund American higher education. As traditional sources of revenue lag further and further behind the need, community colleges, like our private counterparts, seek new, competitive, and innovative ways to maintain and increase revenue streams. While we need to do a better job of com-municating with constituents, we must also build stronger fundraising programs, recognizing that we are not alone in our quest—the competition for private support is increasing exponentially. The *McKinsey Quarterly* reports that there are now more than 1.3 million nonprofit organizations competing for the very same funds.

*University Business* magazine recently reported that it is hard to get a handle on community college fundraising—that much of its information remains anecdotal. Fewer than 10 percent of community colleges participated in the latest annual survey on fundraising, conducted by the Council for Aid to Education. The Council for Resource Development, an affiliate organization of the American Association of Community Colleges, confirmed that while colleges and universities overall raised $34 billion, community colleges raised only $1.2 billion, representing about 3.5 percent of this total.

A recent article in *The Chronicle of Higher Education* states that over the last decade, almost all of America's more than 1,300 community colleges have begun fundraising. These colleges are competing with larger institutions to supplement annual costs and build endowments that will enable them to keep tuition costs low. Community college leaders—especially advancement officers—must incorporate an entrepreneurial spirit and innovative thinking to generate additional funds.

Community colleges, which currently enroll more than half of this nation's first-time college attendees, have an opportunity to attract a larger percentage of these dollars for their institutions. College presidents must lead the way so that college leadership, students, faculty, staff, retirees, and alumni learn to make philanthropy toward public higher education a conscious and important part of their lives.

# Part II
## *Growing Your Team*

Fundraising for community colleges needs to be professionally coordinated and based on a plan "that pulls together the
contributions of all players in an organized, coordinated way."
Michael J. Worth, professor of nonprofit management at the
George Washington University and author of the *Fund-Raising
Guide for Boards of Independent Colleges and Universities*, cautions
that fundraising today is a "professional sport and not a game
to be played by amateurs without proper equipment, experience
and talent." He continues, "In fundraising as in football, it is
best to keep the focus on overall team performance, sharing
both the celebration of success and the responsibility for
inevitable disappointments."

Much of the important work of a successful fundraising team
is completed outside of the foundation office, so your team
should comprise those who have the strongest external
relationships within the community. Your core players should
include college trustees, the college president, the chief
advancement officer, and foundation directors.

### *Trustees*

According to Texas A&M professor Spencer Anderson in
the January 2005 *Community College Journal*, "A successful
community college campaign will not occur without the
involvement of the college leadership in the identification,
cultivation, solicitation and recognition of prospective donors
and sponsors. A strong stewardship process is essential and

should involve college trustees and presidents making donor contacts based on the advancement officer's expert recommendations as well as staff referrals."

As the governing body, college trustees have traditionally been responsible for fiscal planning and policies at the highest level. Faced with a need for resources beyond those funded by public-sector budgets, today's trustees are encouraged to partner with the president and chief advancement officer to secure the fiscal health and identify growth opportunities.

Responsibilities of the college trustees in growing giving include:

- Authorizing the creation of an institutional foundation.
- Exploring and developing new sources of revenue.
- Approving the foundation's long-range plans.
- Supporting the activities of the foundation.
- Serving as public advocates.
- Engaging with high-level donors when necessary as part of a coordinated stewardship process.

Anderson says that along with the college president, having "informed and supportive" trustees and foundation directors is among the top-five factors contributing to effective community college fundraising. Trustees should know that the "success of fundraising efforts is based on the amount a college expends on a budget, in particular on the professional development officer and support staff." Other success factors include:

- The college's public image and reputation in the community.
- The board and president's fundraising and foundation leadership.

## Lori Van Dusen

*Senior Vice President and Institutional Consulting Director*
*Smith Barney, Citigroup Institutional Consulting*

*Chair, Board of Trustees*
*Monroe Community College*

*Director*
*Monroe Community College Foundation*

It was easy for me to support our local community college. Few institutions have the ability to impact lives as well as local economics the way a community college does.

I have seen firsthand how Monroe Community College has changed the lives of the most disadvantaged. Graduates touch many lives–they become our teachers, our technicians, our nurses, our community leaders. The dollars you give to a community college synergize. The impact of a community college like MCC is hundreds of millions of dollars a year.

Those in community college leadership roles know that the funding model is not working as well as it should. Community colleges take on the lion's share of workforce training and development but still serve the traditional student and adult learner. Many young people coming from high schools need more preparation to graduate successfully or move onto a four-year degree program. So, precisely when the demands placed on community colleges are the greatest, we have the lowest level of public support. Private funding is needed more than ever.

At MCC, we have embarked on an image campaign. The board of trustees felt it was important that the community have a greater understanding and appreciation for the role MCC plays, both locally and nationally. Only by educating all our constituencies will we be able to raise funds and serve an even larger role going forward.

- The need for an active and giving board and president.
- A president who is enthusiastic, informed, energetic, open, and involved in the community.

## *President*

The college president remains the vital link between an institution and its donors and is in the strongest position to reinforce the message that today's students are the community's workforce of tomorrow. What an exciting story to tell! From their vantage point, a college president should convey regularly what the community and its economy would be like without a community college—in terms of availability of services, economic vitality, and quality of life.

As principal architect and advocate, college presidents have the challenge—as well as the opportunity—of clarifying the vision of public higher education. By partnering with their chief advancement officer and foundation board leaders, they will be able to clearly demonstrate to prospective donors how private support for their community college will impact individual lives and make the community better and the local economy stronger. The goal is for donors to agree that it is in their best interest to support the college.

Responsibilities of the college president in growing giving include:

- Serving as the college's most visible fundraising presence.
- Providing the central link between trustees and the foundation.
- Developing an institutional vision that is forward-looking and sustainable.
- Ensuring that the chief advancement officer is well-qualified.

- Maintaining strong ties with the foundation board.
- Understanding and being involved in the development process.
- Cultivating and soliciting major gift prospects.
- Attending and speaking at foundation-sponsored activities.
- Ensuring that the advancement operation is adequately funded.

Shortly before the successful conclusion of the MCC Foundation's capital campaign, Building on Success, discussion turned to the next fundraising priority. Because the college's athletic facilities did not meet the needs of a growing student body (over 36,000) and national championship-winning teams, building a field house to enhance the student-athlete experience was at the top of the list. The project would require both New York state dollars and private support to complete. Prior to accepting the challenge, the MCC Foundation Board of Directors partnered with Ketchum, one of the nation's leading fundraising consulting firms, to assess the feasibility of a $6-million fundraising campaign. Confidential interviews were conducted with foundation board members, donors, community leaders, and alumni.

The final report not only encouraged the foundation to proceed with plans to support building the field house but also identified MCC President R. Thomas Flynn as a strong motivating factor. As noted in the Ketchum report, "Those interviewed noted [President Flynn's] strong leadership of MCC as evidenced by his visibility, enthusiasm, and strategic vision for the school. His support of the proposed field house is a significant factor for many in their own support."

## Barbara Viniar, Ed.D.
*Executive Director*
*Institute for Community College Development*
*Cornell University*

The importance of securing private support for community colleges is growing. As we are all aware, the relative contribution of states and local sponsors continues to decline while the demand for high-cost programs and support services is increasing. Add the staggering increase in nonprofits competing for the same funds, and it is clear that fundraising must be high on the list of required skills for community college leaders.

I enjoyed fundraising as the president of Berkshire Community College. Every meeting with a donor, like every presentation to the chamber of commerce, was a chance to share my pride in the college's contribution to improving students' lives. As I was building financial support for the college's mission, I was connecting to other community leaders, not just as donors, but as partners in improving economic opportunity and enhancing our quality of life. Some of those relationships have become lifelong friendships.

At the Institute for Community College Development, we recognize the need for professional education in resource development. Many presidents come to their positions without significant fundraising experience. Their boards may not be accustomed to a leadership role in fundraising for the college, and their organizations may not yet have the infrastructure to support comprehensive development activities. Our goal is to work with experts to prepare community college leaders for success in private fundraising. *Growing Giving* is a valuable resource for these leaders.

Do not underestimate the potential impact your college president can have on your fundraising efforts—especially when their leadership is well regarded within your community.

## Chief Advancement Officer

As the nonprofit sector grows in depth, breadth, and public recognition, chief advancement officers (CAOs) are finding they must work harder to fundraise effectively in a very competitive market. Successful CAOs operate similarly to corporate officers, relying on business savvy and interpersonal skills to establish and achieve goals. As in other businesses, the ability to capture and utilize data to drive communications and decision making will result in the most effective fundraising and relationship-building programs.

Michael Worth notes in the *Fund-Raising Guide for Boards of Independent Colleges and Universities* that in past decades, the chief development officer was primarily a "staff officer, supporting the fundraising efforts of the president. Today, however, most are also front-line fundraisers, soliciting even the largest gifts." In fact, he concludes, the "major-gift programs of some large institutions now resemble sophisticated corporate sales departments."

The CAO should use every opportunity to inform internal and external constituents how important philanthropy is to the organization. Responsibilities of the CAO in growing giving include:

- Engaging and interacting with donors and prospects.
- Collaborating with the college president in order to inspire a vision for the future of the college.

- Serving as the college's spokesperson for philanthropy in the community.
- Developing and committing to a written plan for success.
- Rallying diverse staff and departments to get involved.
- Soliciting top prospective donors.
- Participating in cultivating events.
- Meeting with key constituent groups and identifying their needs and wants.
- Calling on foundation directors or corporate representatives to participate.
- Producing "white papers" to address institutional priorities and plans.
- Remaining visible and credible by attending fundraising conferences, speaking, and writing articles.

Effective CAOs balance the strategic plan of the college with the expressed needs of donors. By engaging prospective donors early, professional fundraisers are able to learn more about the donor's personal values and "agenda" for giving. This enables the CAO to identify opportunities and navigate effectively to satisfy the needs of both the donor and the college–setting the stage for continued, positive interaction.

## Foundation Directors

As nonprofit corporations, community college foundations solicit, receive, and disburse private funds and derive their authority and legitimacy from the institutions with which they are affiliated. A foundation needs to balance its autonomy with an appropriate degree of accountability to its governing board.

> *Today's environment...requires*
> *board members who are strongly*
> *committed to an institution.*

In earlier years, community college foundation boards were socially oriented. Board giving was welcomed, but less critical, back in the days when state and local funding adequately met a college's needs. In contrast, today's highly competitive philanthropic environment requires board members who are strongly committed to an institution—manifested in both leadership-level generosity and willingness to cultivate prospects for giving.

Nonprofit organizations have larger boards than for-profit organizations for good reason. In a study about why the wealthy give, 43 percent indicated that their significant contributions went to organizations where they sat on boards. According to the *International Journal of Educational Advancement*, institutions where board members were "very critical" to the fundraising process raised nearly $1 million more than institutions where board members had limited or no involvement.

Today's board members are looking for positive experiences. In June 2005, the *Deloitte Volunteer Impact Survey* (of employed Americans) found that 86 percent felt that board service and volunteering had a positive impact on their careers; 78 percent stated that it helped to develop business skills; and 73 percent stated that it enhanced leadership abilities. Providing such outcomes may require an action plan to make your board attractive to community and business leaders.

**James J. Ward**
*Vice President (retired)*
*Bausch & Lomb*

*Development Chair*
*Past Board Chair, 1998-2002*
*Monroe Community College Foundation*

Philanthropy started at an early age for me. The concept of "You always get back more than you give" has proven true in my life. The many opportunities and mentors have taken a kid from the streets of Philadelphia through graduate school and a successful financial career. Giving back to the community and those in need with financial and direct support balances my life's objectives. It just makes sense.

In its short 40-year history, Monroe Community College has earned the respect and admiration of employers and civic leaders. MCC provides a broad list of programs that meet both traditional student needs as well as specific training that supports the community's infrastructure services. You can't go through a day without being serviced by someone educated or trained at MCC.

The MCC Foundation was developed in 1982 to help fund both college growth and student scholarships. The foundation's support has escalated over the years as public funding has diminished. Private funding is becoming increasingly essential as the needs of the college and the community continue to expand and government support continues to decline.

The unified approach to fundraising between the college and the foundation continues to be successful and inspirational to all the trustees, foundation directors, and the many volunteers. It makes everyone want to go the extra mile.

Understandably, the influence and effectiveness of a foundation board begins with the reputation, capabilities, and commitment of its members. Although every rule has exceptions, experience teaches that effective board members most often share one or more of the following characteristics: inherited wealth, a tradition of public service, high-level corporate or professional achievement, and a leadership role in the community. In addition, a relationship with the institution, either personal or corporate, is always desirable.

Not every board satisfies the need for every volunteer leader. There must be a good fit between a board, its mission, and its volunteers. A frank conversation with prospective board members can clarify expectations before they join the board.

*Giving USA, A Board's Role in Fundraising* (Issue 4, 2005) discussed the following best practices for recruiting and growing healthy relationships with board members:

- Consider interest, connections, and ability when you recruit board members.
- Orient your board members to your organization's expectations about the board's role in fundraising.
- Build board expertise in financial reports.
- Educate board members about their role in the development process.
- Link new members of the board with mentors.
- Be clear that board members represent your organization, not themselves.
- Coach your board in solicitation strategies.
- Evaluate board performance in fundraising and giving.

The challenge for college presidents and advancement officers is not only finding individuals who possess these skills and attributes, but also recruiting them, retaining their interest, and making best use of their individual strengths and abilities.

To be productive, the foundation must have a viable plan and structure for board activities. This framework encourages the development of strong leadership and shared goals, and it provides the opportunity for the CAO to engage the talents and interests of each member to best advantage. To strengthen a board, the CAO must give high priority to developing effective recruitment, orientation, and retention activities.

Responsibilities of foundation directors in growing giving include:

- Demonstrating strong interest and commitment to the college and its foundation.
- Assisting in carrying out the board's fiduciary responsibility.
- Leading by example by personally investing in the college and its programs.
- Participating in board meetings.
- Becoming knowledgeable about the college and its mission.
- Acting as ambassadors for the college.
- Identifying, cultivating, and soliciting potential donors in the private sector.
- Hosting or attending foundation-sponsored events and activities.
- Recommending and cultivating prospective board nominees.

**Leonard Redon**
*Vice President*
*Paychex Inc.*

*Immediate Past Chair*
*Monroe Community College Foundation*

At times I am asked why I have devoted so much of my energy and resources to Monroe Community College. I am not a graduate, nor are my wife or children. Actually, the answer to this question is quite clear to me. First, as a business leader in our community, I came to realize what an important asset MCC is to our community. Its ability to be responsive to specific business training and educational needs helps local companies compete on a global scale. It also is responsive to more topical requirements like our nursing shortage or training for our emergency responders. In that context, MCC truly lives up to its mission as a community college.

The second reason is that I truly believe that the key to personal growth and the ongoing prosperity of our community and nation is education. MCC makes quality higher education accessible to a broad population that would not have the opportunity in its absence. Single working parents, laid-off workers looking to make a career change, and others can and do pursue their dreams and futures thanks to MCC. In addition, because 90 percent of the students stay in the Rochester area, MCC plays a key role in providing the workforce required for businesses to compete and grow in upstate New York.

When I get involved with an organization, I ask two key questions: "Is the organization relevant in the community?" and "What can I contribute to help it meet its mission?" Relevance has never been an issue for MCC–it refines itself on a continuing basis, ensuring its relevance. MCC has shown me that community colleges are critical to a community's growth and economic development. Any role I have played to help provide scholarships and funding to support MCC has been returned tenfold by the students who use it as a springboard to a brighter future and by the companies and entrepreneurs who employ them and build exciting new businesses that thrive in our community.

Why give so much? I can think of no better way to say "Thanks."

# Part III
## *The Role of the Advancement Office*

The scope of philanthropic activities performed by people in the United States is impressive in its diversity. Certainly, informal and spontaneous volunteer service and philanthropy continue at heartening rates. Nevertheless, philanthropy as a field has developed to the point that many charities and foundations are managed by professional staff members trained in the special disciplines related to this work.

According to *Nonprofit Management Education—Current Offerings in University-Based Programs*, in 2002 some 255 colleges and universities offered courses in nonprofit management, as well as graduate or undergraduate degree programs. As *eJournalUSA* reported in November 2006, "Attracting, managing, training, and thanking volunteers are tasks handled by administrators of volunteer services who may be members of special professional organizations or have specialized certifications or college degrees to support this work."

However, some community college presidents and trustees still question whether fundraising is really worth the effort. If that sounds familiar, it may be time to look at your college's advancement efforts and ask some serious questions:

- Is your fundraising program where you want it to be, or does it seem "stuck"?

- Do other organizations in your service area run fundraising programs that generate better results than yours?

- Do you feel there is giving potential in your community that remains untapped?
- Are your fundraising programs intuitive rather than scientific and research-based?
- Are you less than satisfied with the performance of your fundraising team and/or foundation directors?

If the answer to any of these questions is "yes," know that you are not alone. Many community college foundations have grown only slightly and still produce less-than-stellar returns. Yet, a growing number of community colleges achieve impressive annual fundraising totals. How are these colleges producing such significant results? They orchestrate basic functions to benefit donors, the college, and ultimately the community as a whole.

Danny Thomas said that there are two kinds of people in the world: the givers and the takers. He added that the takers eat well but the givers sleep well. This is, of course, about the givers, the people who "make the world go around." Your success will depend on the people you involve in your cause. I learned that people across the country are a lot alike. And it takes a whole lot of people to find those people who:

- Give because they are motivated.
- Give when they are involved.
- Like to be asked.
- Are not offended by being asked for too much.
- Are influenced by who it is who does the asking.
- Like to know that their gifts are being used wisely.
- Appreciate being asked for a specific amount.

- Would upgrade if there were level-of-giving recognition.
- Enjoy the recognition that comes with giving.

## *Basic Functions*

Advancement offices must work from a development plan, focusing primarily on important, potential donors. Achieving fundraising goals depends largely on four factors:

1. Forming community partnerships.
2. Making the "ask" on a regular (and timely) basis.
3. Having full-time development officers.
4. Responding promptly to requests for information from donors.

Persistent and optimistic, the advancement officer must have excellent listening skills. Understanding your donors' motivation, listening carefully to what they hope to achieve, looking for linkages at your college, and helping to inspire major giving make the role rewarding. The basic functions of your advancement office must work in sync to achieve high satisfaction levels and generate increased dollars for the college:

- **Alumni Relations.** Services, programs, and connections are offered through the alumni office to alumni of record. The definition of "alumni" varies at different community colleges. MCC Foundation employs an alumni director, and the alumni committee chair is both a foundation director and a member of its executive committee. You will learn more about increasing the impact of your alumni relations program in *Part IV: It Takes a Whole Lot of People.*

- **Annual Giving.** A yearly fundraising initiative that solicits college leadership, faculty, staff, directors, trustees, corporate partners, alumni, and other friends of the college for general (unrestricted) support and/or gifts designated to specific departments and programs.

- **Communications.** An integrated communications program that incorporates correspondence, event-support materials, newsletters, and public relations activities to attract widespread, even national, recognition for foundation and college initiatives, promote the activities of your donors, and strengthen the college's visual identity.

- **Corporate and Foundation Relations.** An ongoing initiative that identifies and engages leaders of corporations, corporate foundations, and private foundations in your overall advancement operation. From participating on your board of directors to underwriting special events, corporate and foundation representatives want meaningful opportunities to support the college's important role within the community. Unique giving opportunities, especially those that result in new programs or facilities in response to community needs, need to be developed on a consistent basis and targeted to a specific corporation or foundation.

- **Donor Stewardship.** A program to make donors and friends aware of the value of private gifts is a vital component of private giving. It energizes and informs both the community at large and those who make gifts (Hedgepeth, 2003). Develop programs that build loyalty through recognition activities such as awarding philanthropic medals, prominently displaying donor recognition boards, and naming endowments, teaching chairs, and new facilities.

Since the most likely source of your next gift is the person who gave you your last gift, a donor-relations manager can keep in close touch with donors and friends throughout the

community and organize special donor-recognition events.
A strong stewardship process is essential and should involve
college trustees and presidents making donor contacts based
on the advancement officer's expert recommendations. Sharing
long- and short-term goals regularly and responding promptly
to donor requests for information are essential. A basic component of this position is the art and act of thanking. As is often
said, you cannot thank enough.

- **Financial Management.** A fundamental task for a
  foundation. As the repository for all private gifts to the
  college, the foundation manages and transfers funds in
  accordance with donor wishes, board policies, and all
  applicable regulatory agencies. Accountability is crucial
  to growing relationships with donors. People expect that
  the money they give will be used wisely to make the
  greatest impact on students or community need. Foundations
  must establish standards to justify this trust by setting
  policies and procedures that manifest a dedication to trans-
  parency and governance. In its 2005 *Report to Congress*,
  the Panel on the Nonprofit Sector identified integrity and
  credibility as key to the charitable sector's success. The
  panel stressed that nonprofits must make comprehensive
  and accurate information available to the public and
  implement a viable system of self-regulation and education.

- **Information and Database Management.** This vital
  function captures and manages records on alumni, donors,
  foundations, corporations, sponsors, and other prospects.
  Structure your database so donors can be targeted, and
  include information gathered by continued research.
  This function prepares reports and analyzes all fundraising
  activities, manages the advancement software, and supports

the crucial task of prospect management. Work with your college to integrate systems and facilitate data transfer.

According to Adrian Sargeant and Elaine Jay, authors of *Building Donor Loyalty: The Fundraiser's Guide to Increasing Lifetime Value*, constant access to reliable and current donor information is the key to developing successful relationships. Include in all donor records answers to the following ten questions:

1.  Why did they start giving to your organization?

2.  What are their expectations of your organization?

3.  What (if any) services do they need from your organization?

4.  What communications do they want to receive?

5.  How do they want to give?

6.  How else might they give?

7.  Are they interested in supporting your organization in other non-monetary ways?

8.  What particular aspects of your organization's work interest them?

9.  Who are they (demographic and lifestyle information)?

10. Who and what influences their giving?

- **Management.** An accountable framework for success is important. College leadership must recruit and invest in highly capable foundation staff. Develop a comprehensive manual of policies and procedures to assist in decision making and work flow. Focus staff to work continually toward energizing the board by devising new committee structures, providing extensive volunteer training, encouraging leadership generosity, and closely monitoring

results. Central to the entire management process is a
well-managed information system with accurate record
keeping and timely gift acknowledgments.

In many ways, the field of nonprofit management has become
self-policing, with requirements for annual audits and the
preparation of financial and other reports on results and
administrative practices. Organizations such as CASE, the
National Association of College and University Business
Officers, the Council for Aid to Education, and the American
Association of Fundraising Counsel Trust for Philanthropy
compile this information in comprehensive reports on charitable
giving.

- **Marketing and Resource Development.** No matter
  how sophisticated your fundraising strategy or investment
  policy, the effectiveness of the community college foundation
  is contingent on institutional image. According to Keener,
  Ryan and Smith (1991), important elements in the development of a positive image include:

  Involvement of the college trustees, president, faculty,
  and staff in the community.

  Experience of local employers with students.

  Services that respond to student and community needs.

  An attractive campus, with well-groomed grounds and
  well-maintained buildings.

  The quality of education that the college provides.

The significance of marketing and institutional image is
further reinforced by a six-year study of community college
fundraising, sponsored by CASE. The study found that the
colleges that are most successful in fundraising have two

*Alumni may be especially motivated when asked for a donation by a current student...*

characteristics in common: a strong marketing program and widespread community support (Keener, Ryan, Smith, 1991).

- **Planned Giving.** This program should provide advice and special opportunities to donors, prospects, and investment managers on the fine points of structuring complex gifts to maximize the benefits to the donor. Among the most popular planned giving options are:

   **Bequests by Will**–a simple way to remember those people and organizations donors care about most.

   **Individual Retirement Account (IRA) and Other Retirement Savings Plan Gifts**–help to minimize the tax burden incurred by a donor's heirs.

   **Charitable Lead Trusts**–distribute lifetime income to the college's foundation while the principal is retained for distribution to the donor's beneficiaries.

   **Charitable Remainder Trusts**–distribute lifetime income to the donor while the principal is distributed to the college's foundation following the donor's death.

   **Charitable Annuities**–assets transferred in exchange for lifetime income.

   **Life Insurance Gift**–provides for a significant gift with little cash outlay initially.

- **Research.** Learning about individual and institutional prospects is critical to developing a fruitful relationship with donors. Research will strengthen and support your advancement office's other functions. Create in-depth profiles for serious prospects to help the fundraising team prepare for presentations, and ultimately to ask for a gift. Research also helps to determine whether a campaign to fulfill larger goals is viable.

- **Special Events.** Designing special events to recognize the generosity of individual and corporate donors is an enjoy-able networking experience and provides an opportunity to build relationships with business and community leaders. Strive to create an occasion that becomes the "event of the season" in your community by tapping into local strengths (e.g., popular personalities, venues, cuisine, or cultural offerings) to create an unforgettable experience that will raise significant dollars. Such events will motivate other donors and volunteers to contribute and get involved. Before long, your special events may grow into beloved traditions.

- **Telemarketing.** Determine whether to conduct telemar-keting internally or out-of-house. MCC contracts with a telemarketing firm that specializes in fundraising for higher education clients. Telemarketing companies use the latest equipment to maximize contacts, and they are trained in the art of telemarketing. While volunteers can do some phoning, MCC prefers to involve volunteers in personal leadership "asks" and activities that will generate a greater return.

Professional telemarketing firms also offer higher levels of service–such as script consultation, ongoing analysis, and reporting–to enable you to form better strategies to grow your program.

Telemarketing will generate money, but it is a costly venture—usually based on an agreed-upon number of attempts and completed calls. The best way to get your foundation board of directors, chief financial officer, and college president behind telemarketing is to make a compelling argument that it is an effective method for acquiring new donors. The true value of telemarketing is not in first gifts but in future gifts, or the value of collective giving over time.

Some colleges have a tradition of using paid student-callers in annual phonathons. Alumni may be especially motivated when asked for a donation by a current student—someone whose college experience may be impacted by the gift. As an added touch, have the student-caller sign the pledge confirmation and add a personal note—that might elicit quicker payment. But be aware that students might require training by a professional fundraiser before they are comfortable and effective on the phone.

## *Building on the Buzz: Strategic Communications*

Philanthropy, once the province of the wealthy, is now being promoted more broadly through the media and the workplace. From *Time* magazine's selection of three philanthropists as "2005 persons of the year" to the weekly "Giving Back" column in the *Wall Street Journal* to the proliferation of books, articles, and conferences for those who give and those who get, charitable giving and volunteering are being highlighted as never before. At the same time, community colleges have finally been recognized as "economic hubs," according to Gerardo de los Santos, president and CEO of the League for Innovation in the Community College, places "where the rubber meets the road" and community leaders come for cooperative solutions to concerns.

Build upon the positive buzz that philanthropy is receiving throughout the country through consistent communication with supporters and prospects. Design your communiqués to promote philanthropy, share useful information, and highlight individuals and organizations that have helped to make your development program a success. The following suggestions are key to successfully blending development and communications staff functions:

- **Produce an Annual Report.** Recognize donors, and capture the highlights of the past year as visually and comprehensively as possible. Annual reports provide opportunities to show how the foundation meets its fiduciary responsibilities and manages donor gifts responsibly. Ultimately, your annual report should convey the impact of philanthropy at your institution.

- **Develop and Support a Giving Season.** Develop a theme you can carry through the entire fundraising year that will set your foundation apart from other nonprofits in the community. Your theme should integrate the college's brand and be introduced in the fall as the semester begins. Introduce the theme in your annual report, and then use it to launch the November and December giving season with annual fund solicitations, newsletters, and other media.

- **Use Direct Mail to Support Giving.** Personalized direct mail is an effective tool if used consistently. The 2005 *Nonprofit Direct Marketing Study* revealed that 73 percent of Generation X adults (born between 1965 and 1976) responded to direct mail; 44 percent of seniors (born in 1929 or earlier) also responded to mailed solicitations.

- **Complement Direct Mail with E-mail Solicitations.**
  Distributing a monthly or quarterly e-mail letter to donors,
  especially to recent alumni, will reinforce specific messages
  and help constituents feel connected with the foundation
  and happenings at the college.

- **Stay Abreast of Emerging Technologies.** Keeping up
  with new communication trends is important, especially
  if donors are asking to receive information through new
  media. Are your young alumni interested in receiving
  information via your Web site or a podcast? Should you
  promote your next reunion by sending a text message to
  alumni cell phones? Advancements in communications
  and media pose new opportunities to reach audiences–
  based on their preferences–with tailored messages that
  they will find useful and inspiring.

## *Giving Options*

Now that your development and communications staffs are
working closely together, the next step is to determine how
success will be measured. The most obvious way is to monitor
how many gifts result from your integrated communications
and giving programs. By offering a variety of ways to give or
respond, donors will be able to take advantage of those options
that benefit them personally and satisfy their desire to support
public higher education.

Community colleges frequently offer the following giving
options:

- **Annual Gift.** Any gift, regardless of size, that can be
  expected to recur (and, hopefully, grow) on an annual
  basis. Primarily unrestricted, annual fund gifts provide
  support for current operations, emergency needs, and

other special initiatives. More donors are becoming interested in multi-year annual giving–definitely a trend to follow.

- **Capital Campaign Gift.** This is a more significant gift given across one or multiple years to support a special fundraising initiative. Campaigns usually focus on a particular set of needs and offer unique funding opportunities and recognition to individual, corporate, and private foundation donors.

- **Designated or Restricted Gift.** These are monies given for a purpose that the donor specifies (e.g., a scholarship, an endowed fund, or use by a specific department or program at the college).

- **Endowment Gift.** Commonly used in education, this is a gift retained, invested, and managed by the foundation to fund an initiative in perpetuity. The "corpus" of the gift is invested permanently; and the earnings are distributed annually to support the initiative.

- **Focused Initiatives.** Support for specific academic and campus-life projects–such as establishing chairs in specific disciplines or developing a groundbreaking program– that draws in expertise beyond the college campus. Such initiatives may provide an added incentive for donors and volunteers to get involved. MCC Holocaust Genocide Studies Project draws interest throughout the region as it brings internationally renowned speakers to its programs, and donors to the MCC Foundation. An annual grants competition for faculty and staff ensures that innovation remains part of the "MCC experience" and that new ideas receive the funding they need in order to become reality.

- **Major Gift.** This is a gift at a level significantly above the donor's normal level of annual support. A major gift can be outright, a multi-year pledge, a planned gift, or some combination thereof. It provides the donor with an opportunity to connect a family or company name with the institution permanently.

- **Memorial and Honorary Gifts.** These are directed to a program or project or are used for current annual support in memory or honor of someone the donor wishes to recognize.

- **Planned Gifts.** These are major gifts that incorporate some element of deferred transfer of assets, like a life income trust, a charitable remainder trust, or a bequest in a will.

- **Sponsorships.** Also important, sponsorships are private and corporate donations or gifts-in-kind for a special event or annual "friend-raising" and fundraising program. Possible events range from exclusive receptions and elegant dinners to alumni outings and golf tournaments.

# Part IV
## *It Takes a Whole Lot of People*

To generate maximum private support, community colleges must transform their advancement activities to compete in a world that is rapidly changing. New donors, new fundraising opportunities, and new business methods are influencing the practice of philanthropy. As virtual newcomers to the philanthropic world, community college advancement officers must begin by developing a professional case for support to present to corporations, foundations, and individuals–the people who might still view funding for community-based education and training as the province of state and local governments. This is a critical first step.

In *The True Genius of America at Risk: Are We Losing Our Public Universities to De Facto Privatization?* Katharine C. Lyall and Kathleen R. Sell write that public universities in the United States may be at a turning point. They provide useful data concerning the decline in public funding of higher education in recent years as well as insightful recommendations for sustaining these institutions. Together they make a compelling case for the importance of preserving the "public purpose university" if our nation is to maintain its highly educated citizenry and strong capacity for innovation.

## *Educating Constituencies*

So, how do we educate our constituents better? While private foundations and informal think tanks across the country are developing new programs, community colleges can also undertake this role. Moreover, because community colleges have such a broad impact on communities, a variety of options are available:

- Helping individuals with assets and some affiliation with your college to understand more about your institution, the value of wealth transfer, and the potential impact their gifts can have.

- Educating alumni who may be in a position to contribute for the first time.

- Training current students about the philanthropic process and its role in the community.

Community college students can benefit from learning more about philanthropy and the field of advancement. Eugene Tempel, executive director of the Center on Philanthropy at Indiana University, writes in *The Chronicle of Philanthropy*, "It is up to us, in the advancement field, to help our institutions understand the scope of the nonprofit sector, its role in society and the role of higher education to provide leadership in the sector. We have to make certain that our foundations are supported inside our institutions, giving our students an opportunity to work with advancement staff, in the classroom and through internships."

## New Philanthropists

According to experts in the field, more people at younger ages with money and energy to invest are seeking meaning in their lives. "People are looking around," says John Simon, co-founder and managing director at Cambridge-based General Catalyst Partners and chair of the nonprofit

### Arunas A. Chesonis
*Chairman and CEO*
*Paetec Communications Inc.*

*Presidents' Advisory Committee*
*Monroe Community College*

Explosive growth in new and emerging industries, from biotechnology to the Internet, is creating a generation of wealthy individuals who bring to philanthropy a non-traditional perspective and equally non-traditional ideas about investing their charitable dollars.

Not bound by generations of family involvement with long-established universities and other nonprofits, these new philanthropists are looking for opportunities to help meet the most immediate and compelling needs of their own communities. They offer funds, but even more: They bring a new activitism, seeking to infuse successful marketplace approaches into the nonprofit realm. And America's community colleges now have an unprecedented opportunity to attract and involve such activists.

As one of these new, "entrepreneurial" philanthropists, I urge you to develop a case for support that strongly validates your college's irreplaceable role within the community. Document the financial impact your college makes on the region. Stress your ties to local industry. Highlight academic productivity, innovation, and the success of your graduates.

In doing so, you will gain the attention of business leaders who might know little about community colleges. You'll encourage their involvement; and you'll find them becoming your strongest advocates as you work to grow giving and reap the harvest.

GreenLight Fund (*www.greenlightfund.org*), which funds nonprofit organizations working to address civic questions. "They are looking to do something with their time and money. The question is *what?*" Increasingly, according to Simon, the answer is "doing good."

The timing of this trend could not be better. As round after round of corporate mergers and acquisitions undermine the reliability of corporations as sources of philanthropic dollars, wealthy individuals, many from the venture capital world, are becoming increasingly important to nonprofit organizations as sources of both money and knowledge.

The new breed of philanthropist is not content to just write a check at the end of the year. These individuals tend to be focused in their giving, and they often want a clear picture of how their time, skills, and passion can create the greatest impact. "It's not just writing a check and hoping something good happens," said Paul Grogan, president of the Boston Foundation (*www.tbf.org*). It's about asking, "Is there going to be a return on investment, and how will I know?"

People with new wealth bring a different perspective to philanthropy. Giving at younger ages than did their parents' generation has set these new philanthropists on the course to give throughout their lives. They want to be informed about, and highly engaged with, the charities they support. While their gifts are often made independently, sometimes they give in groups through "giving circles" (discussed later in this section) or community foundations to make a more visible and recognized impact. However, while they may possess tremendous wealth, they are not as generous as their older counterparts, according to a study by New Tithing Group, a San Francisco nonprofit that encourages people to give more to charity. Surprisingly, New Tithing reports that Americans earning $50,000 to $100,000 annually give two to six times more than those who make more than $10 million.

Economic prosperity has resulted in a dramatic proliferation of foundations, according to *JournalUSA*. The few thousand post-World War II American grant-making institutions have swelled today to more than 65,000 organizations worldwide, testifying to the profound growth in philanthropy–not just in the United States, but on a global level. The assets of these foundations now total more than $500 billion, with giving at an all-time high of $33.6 billion annually. "While many wealthy people make direct, individual donations to causes that they particularly support, many, and especially those in the public eye, may also choose to establish a foundation to handle their contributions. This shields a prominent person from direct appeals for support and allows large funds and endowments to be professionally managed. Whether financed by and directed toward, the interests of one person or a family, or reflecting the concerns and utilizing the resources of a long-ago individual or corporate source, foundations disperse funds, often through grants, to support many vital programs and constituencies."

The MCC Foundation has been successful in engaging the newly wealthy by tailoring its approach to meet their needs. Family and business interests are rigorously researched before making an approach. A request for support is positioned as an investment that will produce long-term benefits for both the donor and the college. Gift proposals are designed to be

### Mary Virginia Porcari Keough
*Community Volunteer*
*The Brady Fund*

### Charles F. Porcari
*Director of Public Affairs*
*American Federation of Teachers*
*The Brady Fund*

The grieving process following the sudden loss of our mother—a woman who during her life counseled others in that process—was, frankly, not cutting it for us. We, the four surviving children of Mary Porcari Brady, a 1972 graduate of Monroe Community College, were searching for something more. Our mother had attended class, graduated, and subsequently embarked on a career as a registered nurse, all while raising four kids. Her lessons were not spoken but rather communicated through example: Service above self, assistance for those less fortunate than you, and ultimately, the notion of something greater than yourself.

We turned to MCC with our first conversation about wanting to do something more. While life and circumstances had taken the four of us away from Rochester and MCC, we knew from the start that MCC would be the integral part of anything we were able to do. The reason was simple: Our mother loved MCC and loved the life her education there helped her achieve.

**James A. Porcari**
*President, Personal Lines Claims Division*
*AIG Corporation*
*The Brady Fund*

**John D. Porcari III**
*Secretary*
*Maryland Department of Transportation*
*The Brady Fund*

We approached the MCC Foundation and asked them what they needed to bolster their nursing program. Extraordinarily helpful from the start, MCC offered us a range of philanthropic options, including one–which we ultimately selected–where they identified through staff consultation a need they had never addressed before: an emergency student-support fund.

The Monroe Community College Foundation staff were not sales people; they were "challenge solvers." They approached our desires with an open mind, without any hidden agendas. As amateur philanthropists, we sought not kudos and reinforcement, but rather answers and options. Given a challenge to be creative, MCC came up with a phil-anthropic option that met our family's desires, one that today stands as all we had hoped when we embarked on this mission to honor Mary Porcari Brady's memory.

informative, unique, and concise while providing giving options. Appealing benefits are offered, such as naming opportunities, public recognition, networking opportunities, committee involvement, and prestige. Whenever possible, requests are timed to business events, such as sales, consolidations, and stock executions.

When working with the newly wealthy, it is important to provide longer lead times to enable the donor to carefully consider requests before making a commitment. New philanthropists are often entrepreneurs who may be short on cash but long on assets, so foundations need to craft policies and procedures in order to accommodate gifts of private stock, negotiable securities, and real estate.

Inviting a new philanthropist to serve on a foundation or college committee that meets their area of interest goes a long way toward making them feel welcomed by the college family. Most importantly, respect their time; new philanthropists often do not respond well to extended meetings, long reports, paperwork, and layers of bureaucracy.

We must continue to engage this huge influx of new donors in our cause by piquing their interest and highlighting the benefits of involvement. One interesting example is offered by the Harper Forum at the State University of New York at Binghamton, which sponsors a breakfast speakers' program for business and community members. Utilizing SUNY Binghamton's faculty—and at times national speakers—the forum provides an elite networking opportunity, gives participants the chance to know the college on a more personal basis, and unites the community and the campus.

It is important to remember that new philanthropists are more demanding–requiring more time and cultivation–and have much to say about the fundraising process. Many who learned about charity through their families question today's fundraising practices and think of their gifts as investments rather than contributions. Wanting to succeed on the charitable front–as they have in their careers–new philanthropists choose to contribute on their own terms, creating a new culture of entrepreneurial philanthropy.

## *Corporations*

Corporate-college relationships have undergone significant changes in the past decade. While the number of sponsored research and licensing agreements continues to rise, corporate philanthropy has actually declined. This makes the challenge for community colleges that are short on research and long on educating even greater. Today, companies are seeking ways to convert traditional corporate philanthropy into a resource that can help them achieve their business objectives.

Regarding corporate giving, *eJournalUSA* reports, "Businesses engage in philanthropy for a variety of reasons. A primary reason is that a business–really the leaders of the business–believes in a certain cause and are happy to direct resources toward it. There are other reasons as well. Helping the community allows a business' employees to feel pride in their employer and a personal connection to the efforts of the company. This raises employee morale and engenders a sense of affiliation with the company. Another reason is appreciation from the recipients and the community at large: helping is good public relations. Finally, with the system of tax incentives created by the U.S. government, the 'sting' of any financial contribution is at least partially offset by a corresponding tax break."

Curt Weeden, in his recent book *Corporate Social Investing,* outlines an investment model that has become a resource for business executives. Weeden redefines traditional corporate philanthropy by saying that there be a business reason or link for corporate social investment. Thus, advancement officers and their presidents must become more entrepreneurial and seek new ways to leverage corporate support.

- Begin by looking carefully at the businesses in your community to see whether they have resources that can help you. The road to leveraging these resources begins with identifying programs that will best attract their support. Involve your board, trustees, faculty, local business leaders, and community supporters in creative brainstorming to identify prospects. Who are the business and corporate directors and trustees who currently serve on boards? What are the businesses that your students and faculty frequent? Are there companies whose employees you train? What about your vendors? Can you find out the names of the corporate executives whose families you educate? Which companies hire your students?

Once you have identified those organizations, consider the following action steps:

- Research the interests and activities of the companies.
- Check within your institution to see whether existing relationships exist.
- Determine whether your project will appeal to a number of companies or mesh with the interests of just one.

### Joseph M. Cahalan, Ph.D.
*President*
*The Xerox Foundation*

We don't donate to Monroe Community College, we invest in it. It is one of the best social investments we make year-in and year-out. MCC and Xerox have grown up together. Although the first MCC class was enrolled in 1962, the idea of the college was born in 1960–the same year that Xerox announced the world's first plain-paper copier and one of the most successful inventions of the 20th century. Since those early days, our two institutions have enjoyed a remarkably robust and beneficial partnership.

Over the past three decades, we have invested some $3 million in MCC. It's been returned to us many times over–by the thousands of alumni who have joined our company, by strengthening the labor pool from which we recruit, by honing the skills of our employees, by playing a critical role in making the community stronger, and by standing as a source of pride for all Xerox people.

We consider our relationship with the college to be a strategic partnership. Like all good relationships, it serves the interest of both parties. We invest human and financial resources in the college, and the college plays a critical role in developing our work force.

The people of MCC work hard to make the partnership work. They hire the best, develop them to their maximum potential, and keep them for long periods of time. They understand our needs and ambitions and work with us to help achieve them. They interact with us as one entity, not

an array of schools and departments. In other words, they
practice the lessons put forth in this book.

Xerox has just survived the worst financial crisis in our history–
a crisis that had us teetering on the brink of bankruptcy. In
2000, we lost $273 million; in 2005 we made $978 million.
The single biggest reason for our turnaround was the quality
and loyalty of our people. MCC plays a critical role in
nurturing that quality and loyalty. If the college didn't exist,
we would have to create it.

- Be prepared to discuss a variety of ways that the company
  can assist you (e.g., do they have space you can rent,
  knowledge they can share, internships to offer, or useful
  goods or property that they can contribute?)
- Determine whether it is appropriate to extend recognition
  for their contributions (i.e., naming rights or other
  recognition).

Creative thinking–beyond the traditional gift of cash, grants,
and contributions of material support–will empower donors
to make a more personalized decision to support your college.
Match their generosity by announcing the gift publicly and
by promoting its impact in such a way that it helps to build
or reinforce their reputation and market their business within
the community or beyond.

Brite Computers, headquartered in Rochester, NY, sought
to introduce new 3-D display systems to the college market.
Chair and CEO John Smith, an alumnus, donated two systems
(servers, software, and display screens totaling $37,000 each)
to the colleges he attended: MCC and Rochester Institute
of Technology. The gift enhanced the learning experience for

the college students within faculty innovations centers (MCC) and animation and industrial design classrooms (RIT), but it also provided Brite Computers with valuable case studies to use to launch the product nationwide.

While creative approaches require time and energy, it essential to take the time to broaden relationships with corporate leaders. If successful, you will develop long-term partnerships that will enhance your prospects for future gifts. Moreover, corporate participation will create a role model for other companies.

Remember to conclude your solicitation with a gentle reminder that by supporting your college, they are partnering with other successful businesses, reaching new markets, and, of course, getting access to your institutional leadership.

## *Current Donors*

A recent article in *The Chronicle of Higher Education* states that the learning curve facing most advancement professionals in two-year institutions is steep. We must do a better job of educating ourselves–especially by learning more about our current donors and better understanding their giving behaviors.

In their excellent book *Building Donor Loyalty*, Adrian Sargeant and Elaine Jay identify a variety of factors that motivate donors to give: self-interest, sympathy, empathy, a belief in social justice, and a desire to follow social norms. The key is in taking the time to understand more about what prompted donors, current and past, to make their first gift and build upon that motivation. Were they merely asked through a phone call or a letter, and did they respond because of some connection? If so, was it because they were imbued with a sense of giving from an early age? Did they become involved through service as a board member or trustee, or on an advisory committee? Did they have other interactions with the college or its students? Did a friend ask them to give?

The Forum of Regional Associations of Grantmakers (*www.givingforum.org*) discovered that just like the newly wealthy, today's donors want more direct involvement with an organization before making their second gift, and they report that the closer they feel to your institution, the more they will give. Many express misgivings and misunderstandings about operations, and say they "want money to go directly to people in need." Some do not see the connection between organizational infrastructure and effective fundraising.

Donors who become involved and committed are the most generous. Syracuse University Professors Arthur C. Van Slykes and David M. Brooks report in an article in *The American Review of Public Administration* that volunteerism does not replace giving, but instead enhances it. It is an important lesson that we must all remember.

Seventy-five million baby boomers (born between 1946 and 1964) will be retiring in this decade. According to a recent study by the Pew Research Center entitled *From the Age of Aquarius to the Age of Responsibility* (December 2005), baby boomers are expected to provide a pool of volunteers for nonprofit work. Volunteering is the best way for new donors to get to know you and your institution, so consider recruiting these baby-boom retirees as volunteers. If they receive satisfaction from this relationship, they will be inspired to support your institution.

With 85 percent of American private giving coming from individuals, it is wise to begin or enhance a donor-education program at your community college. The engagement of donors–commonly referred to as stewardship–moves the donor-institutional relationship forward. Stewardship may take a variety of forms:

- Asking donors to serve on committees at the college or foundation.
- Ensuring that timely, personalized acknowledgments are sent for each gift.
- Educating donors on college goals and strategic initiatives.
- Highlighting how their contributions made a difference.
- Welcoming them into a giving circle or leadership society.
- Inviting them to special events and seminars.
- Providing clear and concise financial reporting.
- Delivering consistent and meaningful communications.

Time and again, donors comment that meeting scholarship recipients and receiving personal thank-you letters is very meaningful and appreciated. Require students to write thank-you letters to donors as part of the scholarship agreement, and provide them with preferred contact names, addresses, and some background information about the donor if available. Consider hosting a reception that brings together scholarship recipients and benefactors each year so students can convey in person how the scholarship has helped them achieve their goals and perhaps changed their life. Experience shows that donors who meet those individuals who have benefited directly from their generosity are more likely to give again and promote your efforts to others.

In *Independent Sector, The Stages of Giving* (1999), former chair and CEO of Hudson Corporation Kenneth Dayton describes the personal stages of giving, based on his personal experiences with philanthropy:

- **Minimal Response.** Giving only when asked.
- **Involvement and Interest.** Donors believe in the cause and want to make it better. Giving becomes meaningful and purposeful.
- **As Much As Possible.** A major transformational breakthrough that requires thinking, a budget, and priorities.
- **Maximum Allowable.** The IRS five-year carry-forward provision allowed donors to plan and to think creatively about philanthropy, including the opportunity to initiate projects.
- **Beyond the Max.** Donors disregarded the IRS maximum and began to give what they wanted to give. The second breakthrough.
- **Percentage of Wealth.** If one no longer measures giving against income or income tax deductibility, logic soon leads to using total wealth as a measure. Until we started to measure our giving against our wealth, we did not fully realize how much we could give away and still live very comfortably.
- **Capping Wealth.** How wealthy do we want to be? This means setting a limit on your wealth and giving away everything you earn beyond that figure.
- **Reducing the Cap.** We are not there yet. Whether we will ever have the courage and fortitude and intelligence to lower the cap as we get older, we cannot say. But, we are comfortable discussing the subject.

- **Bequests.** Long ago, we decided we had transferred enough of our assets to our heirs. Accordingly, we are able to leave almost all of our assets to the nonprofit organizations we have selected.

We have learned that many of our donors' professional advisors tend to be reluctant to advocate charitable giving. *Doing Well by Doing Good*, produced by the Philanthropic Initiative, Inc. (*www.tpi.org*), reports that many advisors do not have the tools to support philanthropy and thus are reluctant to suggest ways their clients might donate. Educating donors and financial advisors about the significant benefits of planned giving to public higher education is another opportunity to grow relationships.

At MCC, we have created a committee of financial advisors who host regular luncheon forums at the college to discuss the benefits of charitable giving. The forums provide exclusive access to a leading expert—at times representing a local or regional firm—for advice on maximizing wealth-transfer strategies, tax benefits, and planned giving. College retirees, faculty, donors, and other financial planners are invited to participate in the forums, giving foundation officers an opportunity to meet these individuals, introduce them at the institution, and broaden their respective networks.

## Giving Societies

Giving societies are established according to annual or lifetime giving levels. Members of the President's Circle at Monroe Community College (donors who contribute $1,000 or more annually) are invited to a private reception with the college president each year. Members of this giving circle are recognized as leaders in American public higher education whose support contributes to the college's continued ranking among the top one percent of community colleges in the nation. Donors who achieve a lifetime giving of $100,000 or more become members of the E. Kent Damon Lifetime Giving Society, named for an MCC trustee emeritus and director emeritus of the MCC Foundation, and the namesake for the college's downtown campus. The MCC Foundation also manages a society for those who choose to benefit the college through planned giving. The prestige of belonging to the circle or society benefits members and is highlighted in communications, including the foundation's annual report.

## Giving Circles

According to the Giving Forum's New Ventures in Philanthropy, people increasingly are coming together in philanthropic groups called "giving circles." Giving circles, at times referred to as "social investment clubs," provide a way for people to leverage the impact of their giving. The concept of giving collectively as a member of a circle is emerging as a new force in philanthropy. Members of a group, or circle, combine their charitable donations and decide collectively how to distribute the "pool of money" to worthy causes.

Working collectively encourages people to meet their pledged donation, to feel informed about the programs they are supporting, and to feel that they are making a big enough donation to make a difference or send a message. This collective empowerment appeals to many audiences, especially those

> *...(I)t makes sense to begin*
> *cultivating students the moment they*
> *walk through the door.*

who fall into the "new donor" category. There are more than 200 giving circles in the United States. Community foundations are examples of an older form of this collective charity.

The Forum of Regional Association of Grantmakers has outlined the common elements of a giving circle:

- Membership is broad, diverse, and inclusive.
- Each member contributes the same amount of money, usually on an annual basis.
- The moncy is pooled.
- Members determine how the money will be distributed.
- The money is used to help address specific community or institutional needs.
- There are opportunities within the giving circle to learn more about philanthropy, finance, grant making, and community issues.
- The membership is proactive and participatory.
- Members provide much, if not, all of the circle's administrative support.

Giving circles usually begin with an informal gathering organized around a particular issue or area of interest (e.g., the environment, human rights issues, or education).

Following are some simple steps toward forming effective giving circles:

- Identify an individual to invite ten peers to an organizational meeting.
- Use the group's feedback to determine the group's focus.
- Suggest options for giving and giving guidelines.
- Research and recommend projects and activities of interest.
- Solicit applications, and make awards.

This concept can be expanded to retirees, current faculty, parents and grandparents, and families; it is an excellent way to get more individuals involved while reinforcing relationships between peers.

## Students

Community colleges—which collectively have educated millions of citizens—have a unique opportunity and obligation to teach students about today's philanthropic challenges and rewards. Students should be exposed to the role of philanthropy in the life of the institution as early as possible during their academic careers.

If community college advancement programs are to succeed at fundraising, it makes sense to begin cultivating students the moment they walk through the door. A recent survey conducted by the University of California-Los Angeles reports that first-year undergraduates' interest in performing community service and assisting the needy has surged. The 2005 survey—based on polls of 263,710 freshmen at 385 of the nation's four-year schools—found that 66.3 percent believe it is very important or essential to help others in difficulty. That figure is up from 62.4 percent in 2004 and represents the highest percentage in 25 years. In addition, 26.3 percent said there was a "very good" chance they would participate in volunteer or community service while in college–up from 24.1 percent in 2004 and the highest since researchers began asking that question in 1990. In all, 67.3 percent of freshmen said there was at least "some" chance they would do such work. These and other findings in the survey demonstrate that the 2005 freshman class "cares about civic and social responsibilities," said Pryor. There is no time like the present to connect with students and reinforce the importance of giving back to their community college.

## Scholarship Recipients

When community colleges fail to teach the concept of philanthropy, they are missing the opportunity to grow student gift programs and alumni participation. Advancement teams must correct negative impressions of fundraising and engage students while they are still at the college.

Since more than one-third of all community college students receive some type of aid, students should be made aware of how private support helped them to pursue their education. Scholarship recipients should know as much about their donors as possible. Since receiving a scholarship or other form of support occurred at an impressionable time in their lives, it offers an important opportunity to reinforce their future obligation to help other students. Most advancement officers attest that successful scholarship recipients often prove to be the most dependable benefactors. Even though federal and state governments are heavily involved in student financial aid, philanthropy creates real opportunities for those who do not have the resources to advance their own or their children's education.

The following suggestions are ways to engage students in a conversation about philanthropy:

- Produce a brochure to introduce the foundation to current students.

- Develop a section of your Web site that serves the needs of students.

- Host new student receptions at the beginning of the academic year to introduce them to the role of philanthropy at the college.

- Establish an advancement scholarship for a student leader, who will then attend and support foundation initiatives (MCC).

- Offer workshops on fundraising or honors-level classes on the subject

- Require an orientation session or seminar on the funding of nonprofit organizations, using the college's budget and financial statement as the central component of the course.

- Launch a welcome project–on their first night as freshman in the residence hall, when you can leave a small gift from the alumni association on their pillow along with a card welcoming them to the college and looking forward to their eventual membership in the alumni association (SUNY Binghamton).

- Invite a student to serve on your foundation's board of directors to represent the voice of the current generation

and serve as a liaison to the student body (Virginia
Community College System).

- Ask students to contribute at least $5 toward an emergency
  scholarship fund–students will have a greater appreciation
  of donors' generosity if they, too, invest in their own
  futures (Lord Fairfax Community College Foundation).

- Employ students in the advancement office.

- Establish a "philanthropy council," comprising students
  selected and trained in development and event planning.

- Ask successful students to speak at foundation board
  meetings and at special events.

- Develop a student-funding initiative to support a college
  program or scholarship.

- Build recognition by noting that the source of each
  scholarship is your foundation.

Closer to graduation, consider activities that will connect
students and alumni from your institution. According to Randy
Randall, executive director of alumni and community relations
at Presbyterian College, "Commencement signifies the end
of the student phase of life–and can help create excitement
about moving into the alumni phase of involvement." The
following suggestions will help students make the transition
to active, supporting alumni:

- Host a graduation picnic to introduce students to
  the alumni association.

- Hand out ribbons as graduates receive diplomas,
  indicating they are now an alumnus/a (MCC).

- Solicit students to make a gift as part of a class gift
  campaign, of an amount of money equal to their class

year (e.g., each member of the class of 2008 would be asked to donate $20.08). The gift may be designated for a specific purpose chosen by the graduating class. Have a class representative present a check to the college president at commencement (e.g., Duke University, Class Act Campaign at Carleton University).

- Publish graduation messages from students and families in commencement programs for a small fee. This fundraising initiative could be linked to a class gift campaign (MCC).

- With the help of student leaders, initiate a student-alumni membership program—a proven way to groom future alumni leaders.

- Create a Student-Alumni Relations Team (START), students who will serve as ambassadors to the alumni community (Villanova University).

- Ask for a lifetime annual commitment at graduation. Track milestones, and at their 10-year gift, invite alumni to increase their pledge.

- Ask recent alumni to return at the start of each semester to greet and provide directions for new students (MCC).

- Involve alumni and students in career-focused events, highlighting one discipline or field per event.

- Connect students with alumni for mentoring.

- Assign your alumni manager the job of student government advisor to encourage interaction with current student leaders. Bringing together the student government association and the alumni association to work together on projects is a win-win situation for both groups (Cecil Community College).

Although community college students lead complex lives and may come from families that haven't had the resources to practice philanthropy, it's well worth the effort to educate them. A study conducted by the Independent Sector revealed that youth who were engaged in philanthropic activities before adulthood are more generous in their giving than those who did not volunteer or donate in their youth.

By demonstrating the role of philanthropy in the college's budget to students early on, you will reduce the "learning curve" when a gift is solicited from an alumnus/a. It should be clear that even students who pay full tuition are subsidized by the philanthropists who helped to build or equip the buildings and created endowments.

Duke University lists among the reasons why students should consider contributing to a senior class gift: "Because attending Duke was a privilege and we're grateful we had the opportunity." Earning a college education is an opportunity that requires private giving in order to ensure that it remains accessible to all who desire its benefits. Your college's mission statement is a powerful message to emphasize within the community and especially as students transition to alumni.

## *Alumni*

From the time Yale University established a means of class-based alumni identification in 1792, alumni-relations programs have built upon relationships among current and past students, faculty, and retirees. Alumni programs keep past students informed about the institution, in contact with each other, and aware of educational and networking opportunities.

Programming for recent alumni is key to the growth of alumni giving. Every expert tells us that the student years and the period immediately afterward are when lifelong connections and habits are formed. It is your job to help these non-donors and recent alumni understand the value of the educational start you gave them.

A 2006 survey in *The Economist* found that charitable giving is flourishing around the world, and that increasing numbers of young, major donors are looking not only to improve the world but also to strengthen the field of philanthropy. Lessons of engagement must be extended to students and selected community college alumni who have the capacity to give. The return on investment will result in benefits not only to our institutions but also to the communities in which we live.

When identifying specific factors that contribute to effective advancement programs at community colleges, Spencer Anderson concludes that, first and foremost, "A successful fundraising program must have favorable alumni relations, the leadership of the community college president and board of directors; and donor stewardship, cultivation and recognition." Referring to expanding alumni programs at four-year colleges and universities, he cites Presbyterian College's Randall, and, identifies the five most important ways alumni assist their alma maters: money, advice, service, new students, and ambassadorial representation. Sharing information, especially alumni success stories and other life-changing outcomes–and getting them published–is absolutely necessary.

Why are recent alumni important? By reaching them right after graduation, you can have them for life. Approximately

**John G. Thompson**
*Chief Financial Officer (retired)*
*Imaging Automation Inc.*
*Member, Foundation Council*
*Monroe Community College Foundation*
*Monroe Community College Class of 1964*

I believe the community college system fills a vacuum in the education hierarchy in the United States. It offers millions of working class people and those receiving public assistance to seek an education beyond high school and climb the economic ladder. I was one of those for whom it represented a second chance to pursue higher education, after making some unwise choices upon graduating from high school.

I was working 60 hours a week to support a family of 6, in addition to attending Monroe Community College. Even given the modest costs, I reached a point where I could not come up with the funds for tuition or books. A small scholarship after my first semester not only enabled me to get an A.A., it gave me a substantial morale boost and an impetus to excel. I subsequently earned a scholarship to a university, to complete my four-year degree.

As a result of this experience—and a set of values instilled by my parents to always help people less fortunate—I have always been inclined to contribute to causes.

I was fortunate to become very successful in business, after which my wife and I made the decision to make a substantial contribution to a good cause. We chose to endow a scholarship fund at MCC because of the impact both the school and a small scholarship had on my life.

I was equally grateful for the scholarship I received from the University of Rochester. However, it is my belief that most private universities have layers of alumni who provide

> much larger and more fertile philanthropic base to tap.
> Community colleges have a much more difficult task.
> However, the need is no less great, and giving to a community
> college probably has a greater impact on people with fewer
> advantages and more challenging circumstances.

58 percent of new donors to the Duke Annual Fund come from young alumni. These donors do not respond to letters but prefer to use emerging technologies such as e-mail, Webcasts, electronic newsletters, podcasts, and highly targeted messages. Regardless of the gift amount, donors should always feel appreciated for giving to your institution. If they feel good about the impact of their giving, they might consider giving again.

According to Randall, recent alumni do not respond to traditional alumni club social events (e.g., dinners with speakers) but tend to enjoy more relaxed social gatherings and service projects (e.g., happy hour receptions, athletic games, or Habitat for Humanity projects). They do not read letters that come in #10 envelopes. His key to successful young-alumni programming is in knowing:

- Who your alumni are demographically.
- What they think about your institution.
- What they want from you.
- How to deliver programs that meet their needs.

How do you gather this information? Stay connected through ongoing communication using the latest technology, assessments, online surveys, and small alumni focus groups.

Research, although at times it requires outside support, will always make planning easier, and programs more successful, because it helps you respond to people based on their needs and wants.

Proven ways to engage alumni in the life of your foundation and in growing giving include:

- Offering them an opportunity to take a leadership role in helping current students (e.g., career counseling or student mentoring programs).

- Inviting them to serve on your foundation board.

- Inviting alumni to events such as homecoming.

- Including a message from an alumnus/a at commencement or having alumni on hand to greet recent graduates.

- Sending a letter welcoming recent graduates to the alumni association.

- Hosting an alumni Web page so graduates can update, interact, and stay involved with the college.

- Sponsoring Web events exclusively for your alumni.

- Surveying how your institution can continue to assist them and acting on the suggestions received.

- Organizing young alumni happy hours in your community.

- Planning a day trip activity or travel program featuring faculty members as guides.

- Hosting service projects.

- Recognizing outstanding professional and personal achievement through an alumni hall of fame.

- Inviting alumni to audit courses at a special rate.

- Providing alumni with a campus facilities "passport" that enables them to use athletics/fitness facilities, libraries, and career center resources.

- Packaging programs for senior alumni, including lectures or events with popular faculty members.

- Offering an alumni philanthropy "101" course to educate them in "wise giving."

- Engaging an alumni prospecting committee to identify new donors.

- Honoring alumni couples who met at your campus.

- Establishing a young leader's council from nominated recent alumni for an annual training program. Based on an effective model in Nashville *(www.ylcnashville.org)*, participants should be nominated by faculty or affiliated companies, show an interest in nonprofit work, and make a commitment to attend all classes. Topics could include board basics and responsibilities, diversity, effective meetings, evaluating nonprofit financial statements, legal liabilities, roles and responsibilities, and special events.

While traditional class reunions might not be attractive to your alumni (outside of key anniversary years), reunions based on co-curricular activities, athletics, and faculty relationships can draw alumni back to campus. Your college might not have a football program—the sport most often associated with alumni weekends and "homecomings"—but it might have a winning tradition in another sport such as soccer, baseball, basketball, or lacrosse. Invite coaches to be part of your homecoming planning committee, and make student athletic competitions against challenging rivals a highlight of your alumni weekend or homecoming.

*Do more to recognize
the young alumni
who engage in philanthropy.*

Be sure to position your Web site as the first place alumni look for information about the college and foundation. Your Web site must be current, provide out-of-the-ordinary elements that ensure return visits, and feature an online directory with the ability to update addresses and e-mails. Alumni expect interactive elements, such as online event registration and online giving.

A donor-acquisition pilot initiative targeting non-donor alumni is underway at MCC. A computer-driven dialing service calls alumni prospects, delivers a brief message, and offers the prospect an opportunity to connect with a live alumni volunteer. We hope that this inexpensive way to reach out to the thousands of non-degreed alumni in our database will break even in costs and acquire new donors for our annual fund.

In a recent issue of *The Chronicle of Philanthropy*, Pablo Eisenberg urged us to do more to recognize the young alumni who engage in philanthropy and do good things for others. "They are the pool of talent from which future generations of leaders will have to come. But they need encouragement, applause and support." Highlighting the accomplishments and generosity of young alumni often will lead other alumni to think of ways in which they may contribute, too.

At MCC, our alumni committee operates as a committee of the foundation board, and the professional alumni director is a member of the foundation's fundraising team. According to the CASE Commission on Alumni Relations, an alumni committee or association must:

- Decide how the association will benefit the campus and alumni.
- Develop programming that is meaningful to alumni and elevates the college in the eyes of alumni.
- Engage with students in such a way that a sustainable esprit de corps is established, building a base of future alumni loyalty.
- Provide opportunities for companies, students, and alumni to see value in their connection to the college and one another.

The University of Maryland Alumni Association has developed popular traditions that engage alumni and current students. The UMAA hosts "fireside chats" and etiquette dinners that aim to prepare students for post-college life. Student leaders are also represented on the association's board of governors and participate in meetings throughout the year.

### Parents

Most parents are staunch supporters of their children's education. While attention may be paid to parents during certain times such as recruitment and commencement, parents are often overlooked as a resource for community college foundations. You may be surprised to find that even though parents may be assisting with, or completely covering, the cost of their

## Richard Warshof
*Assistant Vice President (retired)*
*Paychex Inc.*

*Chair, Board of Directors*
*Monroe Community College Foundation*

*Trustee*
*Monroe Community College*

*Monroe Community College Class of 1968*

After high school, I wanted to attend the University of Arizona, where I could enjoy the great weather, beautiful mountains, and state-of-the-art tennis complex. But the school turned down my application, and I needed a new direction. As I hadn't applied anywhere else, my mother informed me that I was going to Monroe Community College.

I ended up not only liking MCC but loving it. (Thanks, Mom.) MCC is where I learned the importance of a good education, the realities of the workplace, and the value of giving back to my community.

Though I later earned B.A. and M.A. from two other colleges and enjoyed a rewarding career in banking and business, I never forgot the help I had in finding my way at MCC. So I've stayed connected with the college and have done what I can to help today's students chart their own paths.

Community colleges continue to be the best higher education bargain around—top-notch academics at a reasonable cost—but reduced government funding means that students now bear a greater percentage of the burden. With so many different kinds of students—those in mid-career, as well as an increasing number choosing MCC right after high school—every one of us who graduated from MCC can find some-one to relate to. So, now it is my turn to give back and to ensure that MCC will always be available. It is now my turn to help ensure that MCC continues to be there for future generations, for the future of our community.

### Dr. Alvin L. Ureles
*Chairman*
*The Louis S. & Molly B. Wolk Foundation*

In 2006, the trustees of the Louis S. and Molly B. Wolk Foundation awarded Monroe Community College a $2 million grant in support of its nursing program. What were the major considerations that brought about this donation?

Our foundation's overall mission is to use its capital to make Rochester and its environs "an ever growing better community."

Education and health rank among the top interests of our board, and MCC proved to be a perfect fit–a fine academic program with a dedicated faculty; a great track record for recruitment, graduation, and productivity; outstanding, creative programming; and progressive plans for new additions to an already successful endeavor.

In addition, we saw a first-rate administration that focused on our gift, an administration that was efficient, forthright, and grateful.

This community college is clearly dedicated, first and foremost, to educating our citizens at an affordable cost and teaching skills to people who will stay here, raising the bar for the future. It has a serious academic intent with structure and stability, creating better jobs, loyalty to the community, intellectual and cultural assets, and better government.

We are pleased to know that our grant may play some part in this important scenario.

children's education, they may appreciate the opportunity to support the success of the college in other ways.

Include parents in your annual fund program. Start by recruiting a small group of parents to serve as advisors or chairs for your parents' campaign. They will help you identify what matters most to parents and define the benefits of involvement. Parents may appreciate invitations to lectures, performances, or forums with campus leaders where they can talk openly about experiences with the college and be involved in creating the college's future. A nice touch is to offer a welcome reception or special services on welcome day or "move-in weekend" if your college offers residence halls.

## Community

Your college was established because of caring leaders in your community. As such, your college stands apart from private educational institutions because its mission is completely dedicated to the prosperity of the community and region it serves.

Take advantage of your college's unique position by keeping your community informed of the many great things that are happening on campus. Regularly send news releases and story ideas to the local media to demonstrate how private philanthropy is impacting the student experience and preparing the college for the future.

By maintaining strong ties with the president's office and your college's public affairs team, you will stay abreast of important visitors to campus and events that may be of interest to donors and friends. Be proud of the institution you represent, and invite donors and prospects to campus regularly to strengthen their affiliation at every opportunity. If you believe and can prove how virtually everyone benefits from the college's role in your community, offer them a stake in its continued success.

Growing giving opens the door for a community to celebrate the promise that only education can fulfill in people's lives: a better future and a dream come true.

Now more than ever, community college foundations have the opportunity to develop new solutions to alleviate funding pressure by spreading the word that the colleges they support are meeting public needs and providing the link between today's student and tomorrow's workforce. Activities that focus on what the community and its neighborhoods would be like if the college had never existed—in terms of economic vitality, quality of life, and even the people themselves—can help stimulate new sources of support.

Attract to the foundation members who have the desire, the enthusiasm, and the financial ability to benefit your college. Make certain to support experienced advancement officers. Help raise the giving sights among members of the institutional family, and involve them in support of your foundation and its mission. Embrace the college's mission, and convey it to colleagues and community peers to help articulate the need for private-sector support. This will help to validate fundraising initiatives and encourage people to consider the foundation as a solid investment.

Today's 67- to 74-year-olds account for more than one-third of the nation's wealth. And their numbers—and assets—are growing. Many of these wealthy, older Americans care

Henry Pierson "Pete"
French Jr., Ed.D.
*Professor Emeritus of History
and Political Science
Monroe Community College*

*Director
Monroe Community College Foundation*

As an academic, I have been fortunate to teach for 45 years at both public and private institutions of higher education during my career as an historian and political scientist. I come from a family that believes in "giving back"–in fact, my father gave 20 percent of his income and wealth as a "thank you" for having benefited from good fortune. My mother, wife, and I gave money for an endowed chair in his name at Monroe Community College to recognize how far he had come from a tenth-grade education, being a "graduate of the school of hard knocks," as he so aptly put it.

One of eleven children, my father had to go to work early to help support the family. He rose to become a partner in a Wall Street investment firm from these humble beginnings, and thus we thought it fitting that the chair be named in his memory in Business Administration and Economics to encourage faculty to innovate and go beyond their regular responsibilities through a competitive grant process. This has turned out to be very successful in the eight years of the chair's existence.

Five years later, my wife and I funded an endowed scholarship in political science to honor our eldest son, who graduated from MCC having served as president of the Student Association and a student trustee on the Board of Trustees and having lobbied the state capital to encourage support for the college. To date, there have been four students funded with a year's tuition. Each year, our son meets the recipient of the scholarship at an annual Scholarship Recognition Day sponsored by the MCC Foundation.

Last year, after 41 years of teaching and administration at MCC, my wife and I used the unspent proceeds of my unused sick leave to endow an academic excellence award in history, in our names. To date, one award has been granted to honor excellence in scholarship. We look forward to meeting this student at Scholarship Recognition Day.

My father was Henry Pierson French, Sr., I am Henry Pierson French, Jr. and our son is Henry Pierson French, III. The chair, the scholarship, and the academic excellence award have been jointly named the "Three Henrys." We continue to contribute to the growth of each endowed fund so that as the economy increases through investment  we will keep pace.

All four of our children and my wife have studied at MCC. We feel committed to the college's mission and vision, as I have personally seen it grow from 750 to 38,000 students over four decades. Our commitment as a family demonstrates our desire to "give back" for all that we have received through our association with an excellent institution of higher education.

---

deeply about their communities. Many have lived all their lives in the same town and are looking for a way to touch the face of tomorrow. Community college foundations hold a key to their immortality. Tell donors how to endow a teaching chair. Talk to them about scholarships and programs and the people who need them. Excite their charitable interests. Invite them to campus activities that showcase the best of the institution. Introduce them to students. Make them feel a part of the college family.

Working to validate the case for their institutions, recruit volunteer leadership, build new donor constituencies, follow sound board practices, and develop fresh revenue streams, today's community college foundations can play an increasingly pivotal role in funding the college's current needs and long-term aspirations.

A community college's success has its building blocks: notably, a motivated president, a foundation board that is strongly committed, a comprehensive fundraising plan that effectively integrates the foundation's mission with that of the college, and an advancement program that both appreciates and capitalizes on the character of is community.

Colleges must build trust, respect, and confidence with the private sector. The foundation can be critical to this process. Together we must convince our communities that public higher education offers direct and indirect returns on investment that are as dramatic as they are compelling.

There is no question that the fiscal challenges that community colleges face are enormous, but even greater are the risks of inaction. Community college foundations must rise to the occasion and make positive change their new order of business.

# *Appendix* | *Contributors* *(in alphabetical order)*

**Joseph M. Cahalan, Ph.D.**
President
The Xerox Foundation
*joseph.cahalan@xerox.com*

**Arunas A. Chesonis**
Chairman and CEO
Paetec Communications Inc.

Presidents' Advisory Committee
Monroe Community College
*arunas@paetec.com*

**Henry Pierson "Pete" French Jr., Ed.D.**
Professor Emeritus of History and Political Science
Monroe Community College

Director
Monroe Community College Foundation
*hpfrench@rochester.rr.com*

**Mary Virginia Porcari Keough**
Community Volunteer

The Brady Fund
*jinkeough@aol.com*

**Mark David Milliron, Ph.D.**
Suanne Davis Roueche Endowed Fellow
Senior Lecturer, and Director

National Institute of Staff and Organizational Development
College of Education
University of Texas at Austin
*mark.milliron@austin.utexas.edu*

**Charles F. Porcari**
Director of Public Affairs
American Federation of Teachers

The Brady Fund

*cporcari@aft.org*

**James A. Porcari**
President, Personal Lines Division
AIG Corporation

The Brady Fund

*jim.porcari.aig.com*

**John D. Porcari**
Secretary
Maryland Department of Transportation

The Brady Fund

*jporcari@und.edu*

**Leonard Redon**
Vice President
Paychex Inc.

Immediate Past Chair
Monroe Community College Foundation

*lredon@paychex.com*

**John G. Thompson**
Chief Financial Officer (retired)
Imaging Automation Inc.

Member, Foundation Council
Monroe Community College Foundation

Monroe Community College Class of 1964

*raqballjon@wbhsi.net*

**Dr. Alvin L. Ureles**
Chairman
The Louis S. & Molly B. Wolk Foundation

*aureles@rochester.rr.com*

**Lori Van Dusen**
Senior Vice President and Institutional Consulting Director
Smith Barney, Citigroup Institutional Consulting

Chair, Board of Trustees
Monroe Community College

Director
Monroe Community College Foundation

*lori.a.vandusen@citigroup.com*

**Barbara Viniar, Ed.D.**
Executive Director
Institute for Community College Development
Cornell University

*bv28@cornell.edu*

**James J. Ward**
Vice President (retired)
Bausch & Lomb

Development Chair
Past Board Chair, 1998-2002
Monroe Community College Foundation

*jimjward@frontiernet.net*

**Richard Warshof**
Assistant Vice President (retired)
Paychex, Inc.

Chair, Board of Directors
Monroe Community College Foundation

Trustee
Monroe Community College

Monroe Community College Class of 1968

*rswconsulting@yahoo.com*

# *Acknowledgments*

I was recently given the opportunity to take a brief respite from the operational demands of an advancement officer at one of this nation's leading community colleges. A long-time practitioner of philanthropy, I wanted to take a fresh look at this rapidly evolving discipline, to review new models, ideas, and approaches and relate them to the community college environment.

Through meetings and conferences, discussions with colleagues and mentors, and a review of current donor-education initiatives and fundraising literature, I am more convinced than ever that community colleges have an excellent opportunity to grow their giving programs, creating enhanced opportunities for more effective fundraising.

I would like to extend special thanks to R. Thomas Flynn, president, Monroe Community College; the Monroe Community College Board of Trustees; and the Monroe Community College Foundation Board of Directors for their support that made *Growing Giving* possible.

There were many others who helped me in this endeavor. Advancement, after all, is built on relationships, and this project has been enriched by the relationships I have developed over the years. I am grateful to each of you who answered my call.

Spencer Anderson, Ed.D.

Heather Bennett

Polly Binns

Joseph M. Cahalan, Ph.D.

Linnie S. Carter

Brett Chambers

Arunas A. Chesonis

Rosanna Condello

Gerardo de los Santos, Ph.D.

Daniel Freedman

Henry Pierson "Pete" French Jr., Ed.D.

Gail Gregory

Susan Gurak

Royster Hedgepeth

Tom Kelly

Susan Kubik

Mark Milliron, Ph.D.

Cheryl Mitvalsky

Elliot Oshry

Mark Pastorella

Kathy Pavelka

Charles F. Porcari

James A. Porcari

John D. Porcari

Mary Virginia Porcari Keough

Randy Randall

John Rasor

John "Ski" Sygielski, Ed.D.

Karen Shaw

Diane Shoger

Peter A. Spina, Ed.D.

Renée St. Louis

John G. Thompson

Alvin L. Ureles, M.D.

Lori Van Dusen

Christine Van Ness

Barbara Viniar, Ed.D.

James Ward

Richard Warshof

Matt P. Zarcufsky

# *About the Author*

Brenda Babitz serves as president of the Monroe Community College Foundation and chief advancement officer for Monroe Community College in Rochester, New York. During her 17-year tenure at MCC, the foundation has engineered a multifaceted advancement program—focused on leadership development, corporate partnerships, and alumni giving—that has raised more than $39 million in support of college initiatives.

Brenda has authored numerous articles on fundraising and has received many awards for her work in development, community education, and public relations. A graduate of the State University of New York College at Brockport, Brenda pursued graduate studies at Nazareth College and earned a certificate in nonprofit management from Harvard University's Graduate School of Business Administration.

Building on her experiences as a development and public relations professional, she is a frequent consultant and guest lecturer, specializing in working with nonprofits to enhance productivity and effectiveness and address roles and responsibilities. Before coming to MCC, she was director of development and community affairs at the University of Rochester Medical Center.

As a member of the State University of New York's Chief Advancement Officers Executive Group, Brenda works to develop fundraising plans, policies, and procedures throughout the 64-campus system. She also serves on the board of the Rochester Rotary Club, the Holocaust Genocide Studies Project, and the New York State Division for Women, and she is a member of CASE's Philanthropic Commission. You can reach Brenda at *bbabitz@gmail.com*.

**Monroe Community College Foundation**
228 East Main Street
Rochester, NY 14604
Phone: 585.262.1500
Fax: 585.262.1515
*www.monroecc.edu/go/foundation*

*Rosanna Condello, assistant director of public affairs at Monroe Community College, served as copy editor for* Growing Giving.

# *About CASE*

Advancement is a systematic, integrated method of managing relationships to increase an educational institution's support from its key outside constituents, including alumni and friends, government policy makers, the media, members of the community, and philanthropic entities of all types.

The primary core disciplines of educational advancement are alumni relations, communications and marketing, and development (fundraising). CASE products and services are geared to meeting the needs of professionals at all experience levels within these three primary domains.

Practitioners in educational advancement belong to CASE in order to gain access to professional training and networking opportunities, key information resources, and to benefit from the work done by CASE to represent the advancement profession in the United States and worldwide.

CASE is among the largest international associations of educational institutions, serving more than 3,300 universities, colleges, schools, and related organizations in 54 countries. CASE maintains offices in Washington, London and Singapore. For more about the association, visit *www.case.org*.